The Complete
Christmas Book

Jane Bull
The Complete
Christmas Book

LONDON, NEW YORK, MUNICH,
MELBOURNE, and DELHI

This edition published in 2012
First published in Great Britain in 2007 by
Dorling Kindersley Limited
80 Strand, London WC2R 0RL

A Penguin Company

2 4 6 8 10 9 7 5 3
001 – 188422 – Sep/12

This edition produced for
The Book People Ltd,
Hall Wood Avenue, Haydock,
St Helens WA11 9UL

A CIP catalogue record for this book is
available from the British Library

ISBN: 978-1-4093-8060-3

Colour reproduction by
GRB Editrice S.r.l., Verona, Italy
Printed and bound by
L. Rex Printing Company, China

Discover more at
www.dk.com

Christmas

Contents

Have some frosty, festive fun

Let's decorate

Make an advent box and countdown to Christmas. Create baubles and pompoms, mobiles and string things, hanging stars and paper snowflakes to decorate your home and Christmas tree.

Christmas starts here

Open up NO1 and begin your countdown

Christmas Countdown

The run up to Christmas will never be the same again with this 3-D, advent box-calendar. It'll help the days fly by!

Discover the delights in every drawer

No more boxes left to open? It must be Christmas!

HOW TO MAKE YOUR ADVENT BOX

All you need for this spectacular advent box-calendar is one large cereal box and 23 little boxes. On the first of December open the main doors, then each day until Christmas eve open a box to reveal a surprise.

Ask an adult . . .
for help with the spraying

Cut down the centre of a cereal box to create doors.

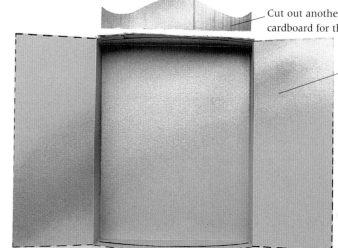

Cut out another piece of cardboard for the decorative top.

Colour the inside and outside with gold spray paint.

Cut out a star and stick it on the top of the box.

Stick flat boxes on the inside of the doors. Check that the calendar can shut properly.

Decorate the calendar with torn-up foil and stick a star on each little box to write the numbers on.

Glue the boxes in place – you can create any Christmas shape you like with them.

SWEET FOIL   TORN-UP FOIL   STICKERS   TREE SHAPES   PVA GLUE

Collect 23 little boxes to put inside

Try out different arrangements with the boxes.

Paint the boxes with acrylic paint and PVA glue mixed together.

Cut doors in the little boxes and use split pins as handles.

Drape tinsel around the box for an extra sparkle, and decorate the star.

Tie on a card star with the number '1' on it.

Open one box a day 'til Christmas!

Fill the boxes with goodies – sweets, jokes, messages, or toys.

Stick down small, plastic bottle tops for handles.

Tie a bow onto the doors to keep them shut.

Write the numbers, on each box inside, from 2-24.

14

Sn❄wy bunting

Deck your walls
with flurries of snowflakes and streamers of happy snowmen.

How to make snowy bunting

The trick with this bunting is to take a piece of string, then thread your decorations onto it with a straw between each one to separate them. Try these simple ideas.

OLD
GREETINGS
CARDS

Take some old cards and cut them into shapes.

Punch a hole in the paper snow.

STRAWS

STRING

Paper snow

Turn to page 26 for instructions on how to make snowflakes out of paper squares.

SINGLE-HOLE
PUNCH

LOTS OF PAPER
SNOW SHAPES

Paper plate flakes

Now make colourful snowflakes and attach them to paper plates, or turn the plates into cheeky snowmen.

HOLE
PUNCH

SCISSO

STRAWS

GLUE
STICK

PAPER

STRING

PAPER
PLATES

PAPER
SNOW

Cut the snowman's face out of paper or card and glue it on.

Glue the paper snow onto the plates.

Snowy greetings

Don't throw them out! Last year's greetings cards make instant colourful decorations. Cut the cards into shapes, punch a hole in them, and string them up with straws between each to separate them.

Thread the snowflakes on the string with straws between them.

STRAWS

STRING

Punch holes in the plates.

Thread string through the straws and the holes in the plates.

Remember to knot the ends so everything stays on.

Baubles,

...stars, and 3D trees

Make them small to hang on a tree

or huge to hang from the ceiling,

but whatever you do, hang them up!

18

3D trees

For a 3D look slot two shapes together. Try two circles as well to give a bauble effect.

1. Cut two tree shapes exactly the same.

Cut a slot in one tree from the top to halfway down.

2. Now cut a slot in the other tree.

Cut up from base to halfway up.

3. Slide one shape onto the other.

4. Stand your tree up, or stick on some thread and hang on the tree.

Paper baubles

If you use old, recycled Christmas cards, all the decorations will be completely different. You could also use your home-made printed paper.

Little or large

String me up and hang me up

How to make baubles and stars

For baubles you will need

Old greetings cards • Thick paper • Ruler • Pen • Scissors • Hole punch • Paper fasteners • Thread

Paper baubles

RE-USE OLD GREETINGS CARDS

RULER

PENCIL

SCISSORS

1 Cut the card into strips

SINGLE HOLE PUNCH

Punch the holes at the bottom and the top.

2 Punch holes

Tie thread around the paper fastener to hang it up.

Clip the strips together at the bottom and the top.

PAPER FASTENER

3 Clip together

4 Fan out the strips to form a ball

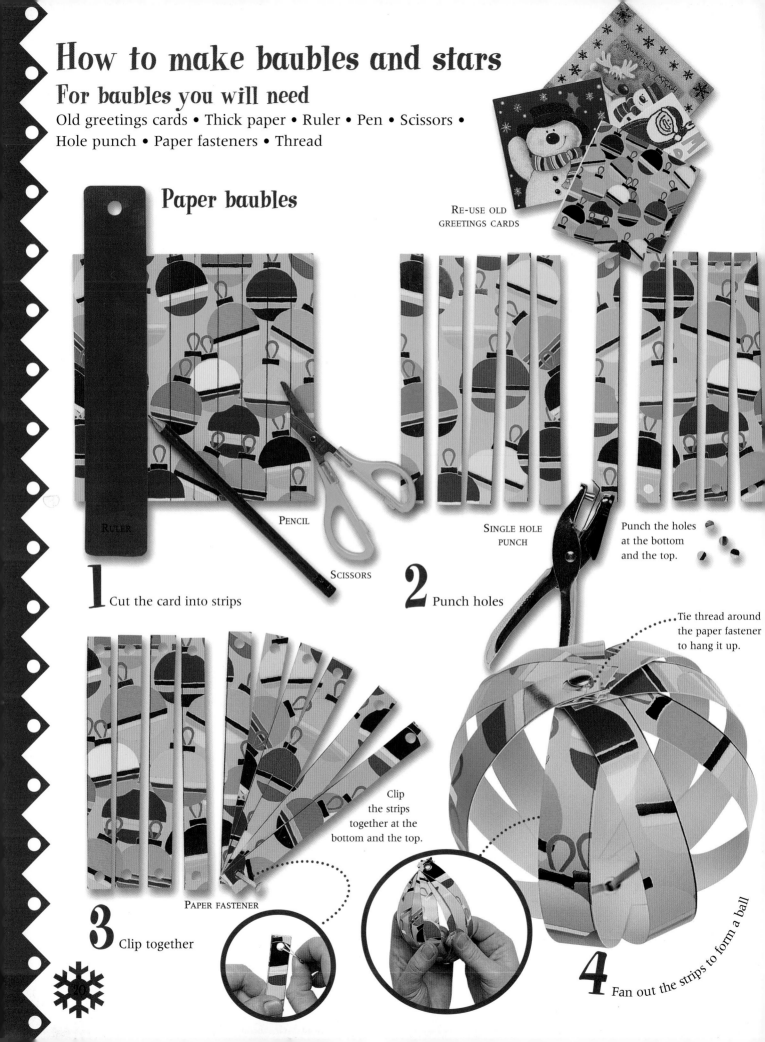

Super stars

You will need:
Paper • Pen • Scissors • Thread • Tape

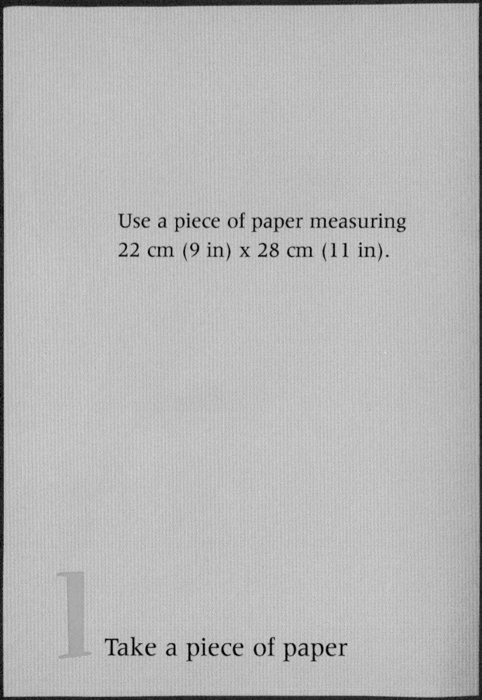

Use a piece of paper measuring
22 cm (9 in) x 28 cm (11 in).

1 Take a piece of paper

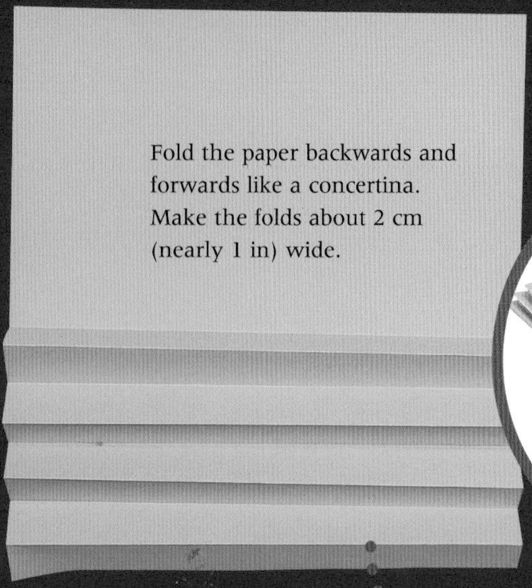

Fold the paper backwards and
forwards like a concertina.
Make the folds about 2 cm
(nearly 1 in) wide.

Fold the
folded paper
in half.

2 Fold into pleats

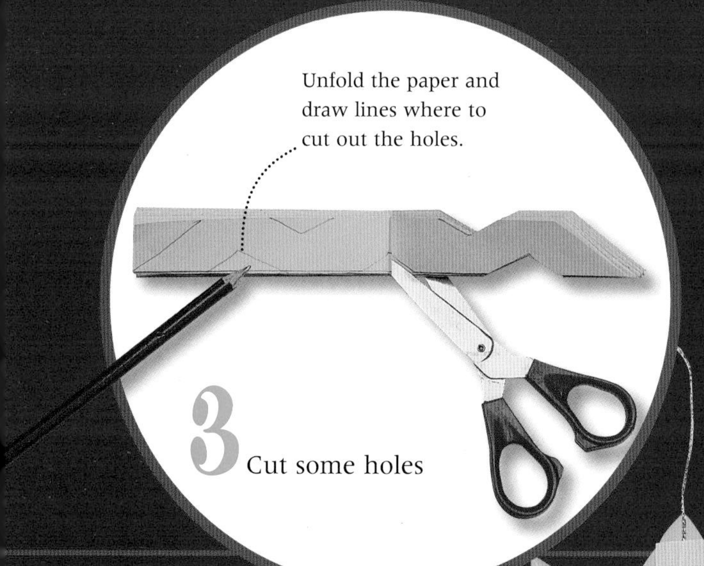

Unfold the paper and
draw lines where to
cut out the holes.

3 Cut some holes

Fan out the paper
and tape the sides
together.

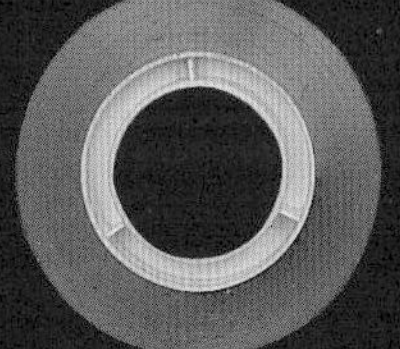

4 Tape the edge

Tape the other side to
complete the circle,
then add a piece of
string to hang it up.

5 It's a star

Winter woolies

Soft and squashy felt decorations

hang around with fuzzy pompoms.

How to stitch some woolies

Collect together colourful felts and threads.
Cut out two shapes, sew them up using blanket stitch, stuff them with something soft, and decorate with sparkly sequins. Turn to page 46 to make pompoms.

NEEDLE THREADER

GOLD OR SILVER THREAD

LOTS OF DIFFERENT COLOURED FELT

SEQUINS AND RIBBONS FOR DECORATION

Needles and pins
You will need:
• embroidery needles – use a needle threader to help you thread a needle
• Glue
• Stuffing

PINS

COLOURED THREAD

PVA GLUE

SOFT TOY STUFFING

SCISSORS

Cutting shapes
To make the templates, draw shapes on a piece of card.

Cover the card with a piece of tracing paper.

Trace over the shapes with a pencil.

Glue a heart to the triangle shape.

Angels and fairies

Cut out, stitch, and stuff

Pin your template onto a piece of folded felt and cut it out.

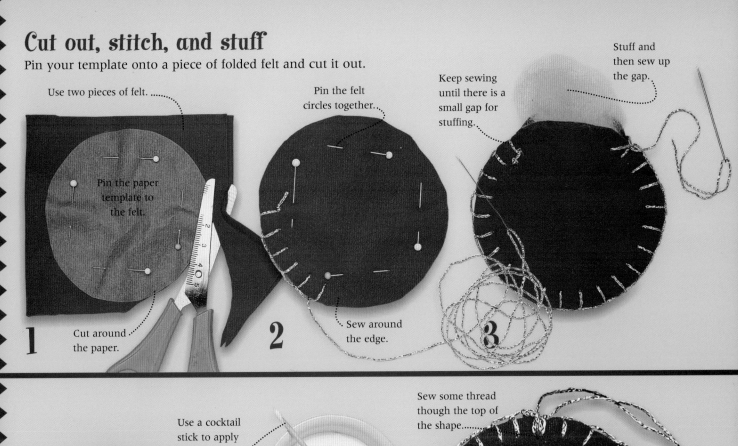

Use two pieces of felt.

Pin the paper template to the felt.

1

Cut around the paper.

Pin the felt circles together.

Keep sewing until there is a small gap for stuffing.

Stuff and then sew up the gap.

2

Sew around the edge.

3

Use a cocktail stick to apply the glue.

PVA glue

Sew some thread though the top of the shape.

Glue on your decorations.

4

5

Knot the ends together.

Blanket stitch This stitch looks great and is easy to do, but keep it neat!

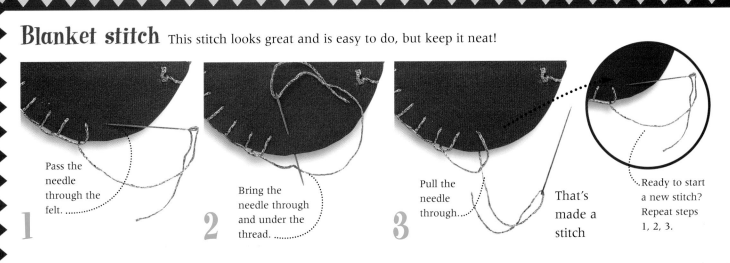

Pass the needle through the felt.

1

Bring the needle through and under the thread.

2

Pull the needle through...

3

That's made a stitch

Ready to start a new stitch? Repeat steps 1, 2, 3.

Paper Snow

A flurry of paper snowflakes

float and swirl through the sky, settling in the branches of the trees.

Take a piece of paper and fold it in half twice along the dotted lines.

Your paper will look like this.

Fold it in half again.

Snowstorms of snowflakes!

Hang up your snowflake with cotton.

Now snip away, then unfold the flake.

See what shapes unfold

Get wrapped up in these paper pompoms

Baubles, Orbals, and Pompoms

Baubles to hang on trees or orbals to hang on ceilings.

28

Transform flat cards into shapely spheres

✨ Hanging Around

Glittering baubles and giant orbals swinging
and spinning around your room give it a
magical, Christmassy feel. All you need are old comics,
gift wrap, greetings cards, postcards, or anything else that's
bright – just make sure you are allowed to cut them up!

29

HOW TO MAKE POMPOMS AND BAUBLES

Paper Pompoms

Pompoms can be made out of any paper you like. Christmas gift wrap is jolly and bright, or you could decorate your own paper with a Christmas pattern using paint or stickers.

Cut out eight discs of paper (about template size below).

Fold the bunch of discs in half and staple down the crease.

Baubles and Orbals

Festive baubles can be hung on trees or simply left to spin from ceilings. When you have mastered the bauble, have a go at the spectacular, giant orbal with 20 decorated paper plates. You'll have a task to find room for something that big!

Take a pile of old Christmas cards and trace around the template.

Cut out 20 circles, and snip out the notches – see template.

Use this template to cut out 20 discs

notch

FOLD HERE

FOLD HERE

Trace this triangle over the template and draw it onto each piece of card.

notch

notch

FOLD HERE

To help you fold, run a blunt-ended pen down the dotted lines.

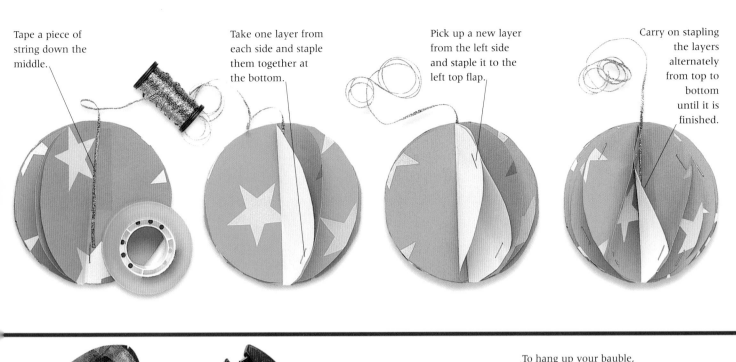

Tape a piece of string down the middle.

Take one layer from each side and staple them together at the bottom.

Pick up a new layer from the left side and staple it to the left top flap.

Carry on stapling the layers alternately from top to bottom until it is finished.

To hang up your bauble, make a hole and tie some string through it.

Staple the flaps together at each end. Keep stapling them together until they become an orb shape.

Make a giant orb using 20 paper plates.

Wow! it's almost as big as me!

Festoon your tree with glittering goodies

Tree Art

There's nothing better than a tree weighed down by colourful decorations to remind you that it's Christmas. Even better if you have made them all yourself.

Turn me into a dangling tree trinket!

Deck the Tree

Ping-Pong angel heads, dangling Santas, glitter baubles, yoghurt pot goodie-baskets, a foil star – they look amazing and are simple to make, too.

Christmas Tree

Turn your bedroom into a festive delight by dressing a tree with an explosion of colourful decoration.

HOW TO MAKE TREE DECORATIONS

Salt Dough Dangles

300 g (10¹/₂ oz) plain flour
300 g (10¹/₂ oz) salt
200 ml (7 fl oz) water
1 teaspoon oil

Put all of the ingredients into a bowl and get stuck in.

Squeeze it together to make a ball of dough.

Cook for 20 minutes
(180°C/350°F/Gas mark 4).
Cool on a wire rack before painting.

Cut out shapes with a cutter or a knife.

Make a base and pinch off pieces of dough to make features.

Don't forget to make a hole in them with a cocktail stick before you cook them, so that you can hang them up.

Ask an adult . . .
to help with the oven

Delicious though they look, these decorations aren't very tasty!

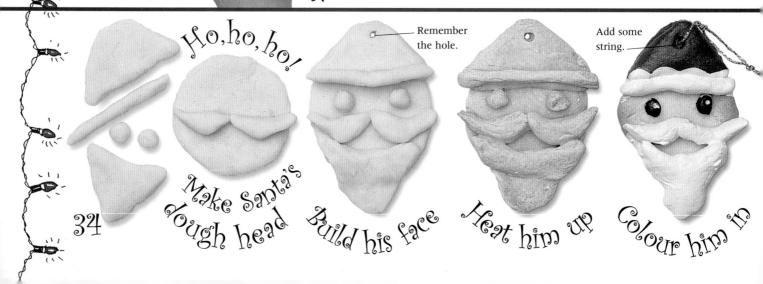

Ho, ho, ho!

Remember the hole.

Add some string.

34   Make Santa's dough head   Build his face   Heat him up   Colour him in

Glitter Card Dangles

All you need for these sparkling dangles is some card and lots of decoration – go wild with the sequins!

Make a hole in the top with a cocktail stick.

Thread some string through the hole.

Draw some shapes on a piece of card.

Cut the shapes out.

Glue on some coloured foil and sequins.

Add more and more sequins!

Angel Head

Transform a cheap Ping-Pong ball into a beautiful angel's face in seconds.

Make a hole at the top and bottom.

Thread string through and knot at the bottom.

Wind string around your fingers.

Tie it in the middle.

Cut the edges.

Glue the hair to the head.

Decorate the face.

Sweet Pots

Fill this doll-sized basket, made out of a yoghurt pot, with tasty treats.

Cut off the rim.

Glue on a ribbon handle.

Decorate and fill with sweets. Yum yum!

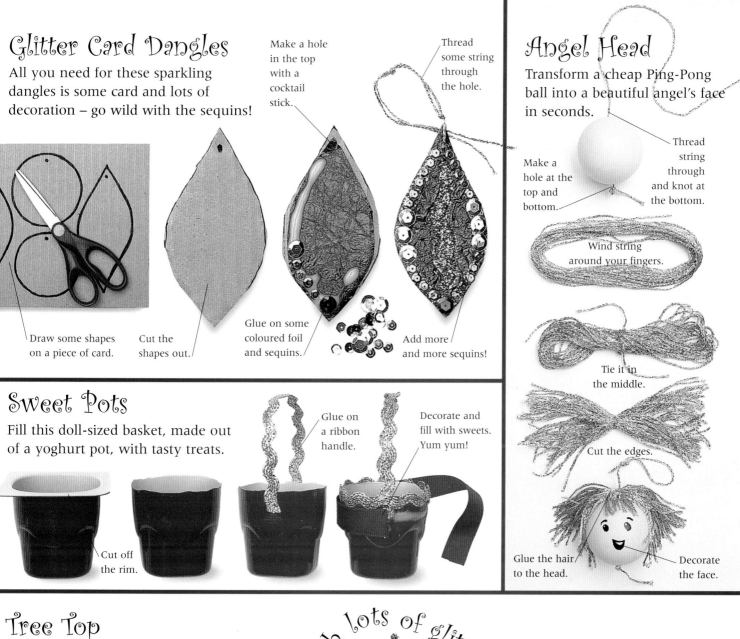

Tree Top

A cardboard star smothered in glittery sweet wrappers finishes off your tree perfectly. Dress up your tree and watch that no-one steals the sweets!

Torn-up foil sweet wrappers.

Glue pieces of foil onto the cardboard star.

To hang it on the tree, attach a band of card to the back with glue.

Festoon your tree with lots of glitzy colours!

Merry Mobiles

Christmas is on the move.

Hang Rudolphs, Santas, Frosty snowmen, and tree faces around your room and you'll be spinning!

Cut out shapes from cardboard and jazz them up

Use cardboard for your mobiles.

Glitter will catch the light when the mobiles spin and give the room an extra sparkle.

Paint the eyes

These baubles make great tree eyes.

Ping-Pong ball eyes.

Give the nose an extra sparkle

Make a hole at the top and bottom, thread some string through, and knot.

Feeling dizzy yet?

It's melt-down for Frosty!

In a Spin

Hang these fantastic mobiles from the ceiling and watch them spinning and twirling around. Remember to paint and decorate them on both sides so that whichever way they turn you can see exactly what they are.

Storm in a Jam Jar

Shake up the snow!

Catch some Christmas magic and keep it in a jar.

Wow! These sparkle more than me!

This penguin feels right at home!

Exploding star burst!

HOW TO MAKE A SWIRLING SNOWSTORM

For your stormy winter wonderlands, all you need are some screw-top jars, water, glycerine, glitter, and a few toys. Add them together, and you'll have a perfect gift for all the movers and shakers you know!

shake, whirl, and swirl!

☆ Take a Jar
Choose a small jar with a very tight, screw-top lid. You may want to test it – you don't want your snowstorms to leak everywhere.

1

2

3

GLYCERINE

WATER

PLASTIC TOY

STRONG glue

GLITTER

⭐ Glycerine

Glycerine is a non-toxic liquid that can be bought in most pharmacies. It slightly thickens the water so that your glitter-snow falls more slowly when you shake it. Use about one part glycerine to two parts water.

⭐ Glue Tip

Use a strong glue that seals even when in water to stick down the toy. For an extra seal, add some glue inside the rim of the lid to prevent leakages.

no great shakes they're easy to make

Glue around the inside of the lid and the outside of the jar rim.

Decorate the lid with festive ribbon.

Stick down a toy

4

Pop the lid on firmly

5

Shake it up!

Salt dough

Four activities in one

1. Mixing
2. Modelling
3. Cooking
4. Painting

Mix the dough and squeeze it into any shape you like. Hours of doughy fun.

To make the dough
you will need

water
200 ml
(1/3 pint)

Salt
300 g (10 oz)

Flour
300 g
(10 oz)

Oil
2 tsp

Put all of the ingredients into a bowl.

Squeeze the mixture together.

Pat it into a ball.

Roll it out

Now have a play!

Make a good impression

Play with your dough

Roll it, rake it, squash it, squeeze it.

Look around your house for objects to press into the dough. You can create all sorts of effects and shapes and if you don't like them, roll it up and start again.

If the dough gets sticky, sprinkle on some flour.

44

Bear necessities

Make the bear shapes.

Stick them together.

Squash a paperclip onto the back.

Bake the bear then paint it.

Tie on some string.

Baking your shapes

Place your shapes on a baking tray.

If the shapes are big they will take longer to cook, and if they are delicate they may break more easily, so keep them small and chunky.

Let them cool down before you paint them.

☆ **Ask an Adult**
to help with the oven.

Bake for 20 minutes
(180°C/350°F/Gas mark 4)

Painting and decorating

When the baked dough has cooled down, you can paint it with poster or acrylic paint. Try mixing a little PVA glue with the paint (about 1 part PVA to 2 parts paint), this will make it tough and shiny.

Keeping your dough

You can save your unbaked dough by covering it in plastic wrap. It will keep for about two weeks.

Save it for a rainy day

45

String things

what a wind up! See-through string balls and fluffy pom-poms, there's a whole new woolly world to discover.

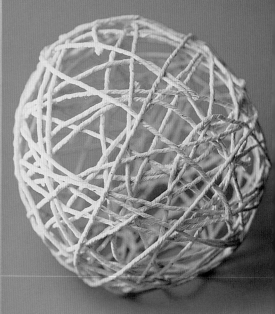

Juggle those pom-poms!

How to make a string thing

You will need • Balloon • String or wool • Wallpaper paste • Vaseline

Blow up a balloon and spread Vaseline all over it – this will stop the string sticking to the balloon.

Mix up a bowl of wallpaper paste.

Cut some lengths of string, about 60 cm (22 in) long.

Dip the string into the paste, then wrap it around the balloon.

Add More and more and more string until you have enough.

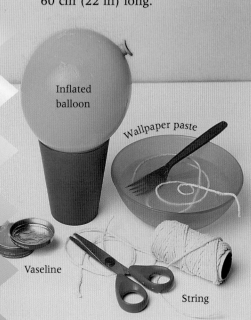

Inflated balloon

Wallpaper paste

Vaseline

String

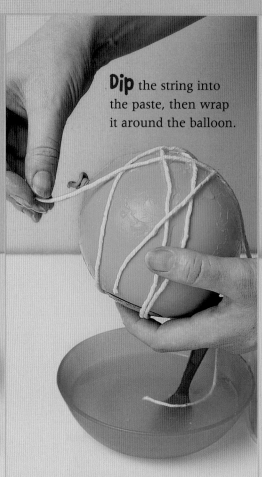

Watch out!
This bit gets messy

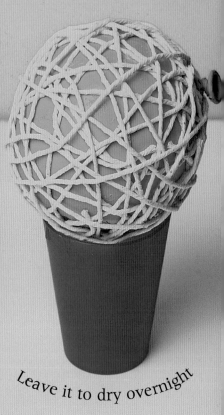

Leave it to dry overnight

How to make a Pom-pom

You will need • Thin card • Wool

Tip: The larger the discs, the bigger your pom-pom will turn out.

Knot the wool in place.

Add more wool until it completely covered

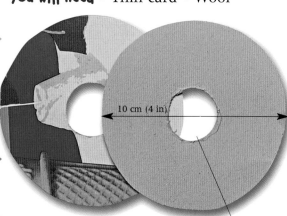

10 cm (4 in)

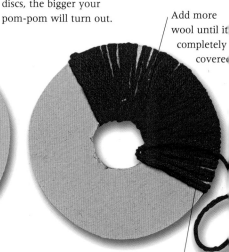

48

Cut two discs from thin card.

Cut a 3 cm (1¹/5 in) diameter hole in the middle.

Put the two discs of card together.

Wind the wool around and around – through the middle and over the top.

When the string is dry...

pop the balloon!

Put the scissors between the two discs.

Tip For multi-colours add different wool as you wind.

Snip away any long bits.

Snip the wool all the way around.

Hold it firmly in the middle.

Open up the discs slightly.

Tie a piece of wool tightly around the middle.

Pull the card off and fluff up the wool.

A pom-pom – it's magic!

Large, small, and rainbow-coloured stars

Hanging stars

These instant decorations are very simple to make and create stunning effects – with rounded edges, for example, they look like flowers. Use coloured paper, or paint patterns on white paper.

PAPER
22 x 29 CM
(8 x 11 IN)

OR for larger or smaller stars, try whole sheets of wrapping paper or pages from magazines.

Fold the paper backwards and forwards in a concertina shape.

Fold the paper in the middle.

Cut across one corner.

Tape these two edges together.

Tape the other two edges together.

Attach a piece of string or ribbon for hanging.

Try all sorts of different paper to match your party theme.

51

Paper roses

Fill a vase with home-grown tissue flowers and give a bunch to your mum.

Wild roses
Create a really wild, colourful bouquet by mixing and matching colours.

To make a rose

Place a plate, about 15 cm (6 in) wide on a piece of tissue paper.

Draw around it and cut the circle. Repeat until you have six discs.

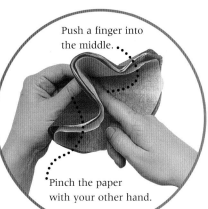

Place the discs on top of each other.

Push a finger into the middle.

Pinch the paper with your other hand.

Squeeze the bottom of the paper tightly.

Tape the paper to a straw "stem".

Rose trees

Rows of roses

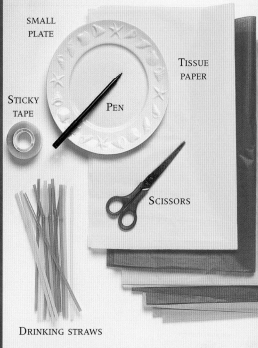

SMALL PLATE

TISSUE PAPER

STICKY TAPE

PEN

SCISSORS

DRINKING STRAWS

Perfect petals

Finally, pull the layers apart carefully to fluff up the flower.

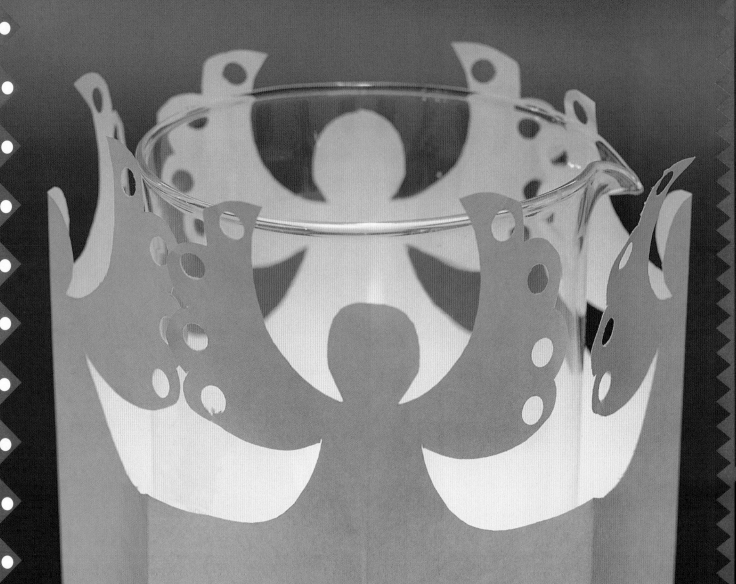

Christmas night

Hush now, all is quiet.

Light your lanterns and watch them twinkle in the dark to welcome festive friends.

Alternatively glue tissue paper circles onto your tracing paper.

3
Tissue paper
Cut out some blue tissue paper the same size as the tracing paper, draw on stars, and cut them out.

2
Cut out a landscape from coloured paper and glue it to the tracing paper.

4
Glue the blue paper to the back of the tracing paper.

Festive forest

1
Cut some tracing paper to fit around a jar.

5
Wrap the sheet around the jar.

Tape in position.

Shining star jar

1 Cut a piece of paper the height of the jar and long enough to fit around it.

2 Snip a zigzag along the top and draw and cut a pattern out of the middle.

3 Glue a different-coloured piece of tissue paper to the back of the design and wrap the paper around the jar.

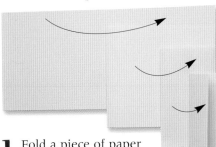

Glowing angels

1 Fold a piece of paper in half then half again and again.

Draw a design on the folded paper, and cut it out.

2 Unfold the paper.

3 Make the paper into a crown shape and tape the ends together. Slip it over a large jar.

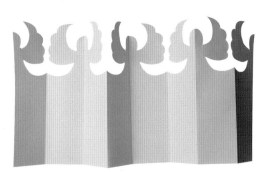

This design slips over a jar – it's not attached like the others.

57

Festive windows

Day and night give your room a Christmassy glow
with these tissue paper windows

1

SCISSORS

PENCIL

Draw your picture on a sheet of
dark-coloured card, and cut out
some shapes.

2

Glue pieces
of tissue to
the back of
the picture.

GLUE
STICK

COLOURED
TISSUE PAPER

3 Turn your picture
back over.

Now stick your silhouette
in the window and let
it shine out!

Clever cut-outs

Instead of a picture, try cutting out a snowflake from folded paper. Turn to page 26 to find out how to make one.

A flurry of snowflake windows.

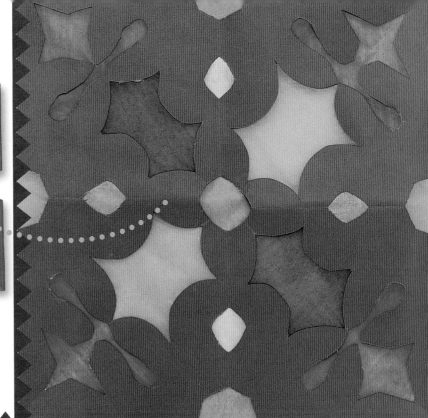

59

Christmas scents

Sweet and spicy mixes of cinnamon and cloves with the fruity aroma of orange fills the air.

Pomanders and pot pourri – perfect to give as presents.

Making scents

Rich, spicy smells are all around at Christmas time, so why not collect them up and bottle them.

Pour in the ingredients

Mix up a pot of scents

To make pot pourri, spoon spices, such as ground nutmeg and mixed spice, into a jar. Then add cinnamon sticks, nutmegs, cloves, etc. to fill it. Turn the jar over to mix it up and keep it in a cool, dry place. Keep turning it once a day for four weeks.

Place on the lid.

Turn the jar each day.

Keep turning for weeks.

CINNAMON STICKS

ORRIS ROOT

MIXED SPICE

NUTMEGS

ALLSPICE BERRIES

STAR ANISE

Clove-studded oranges

These scented fruit are called pomanders. Oranges work best but you could try other citrus fruits as well. The jewelled pomander will last only a few days but the clove-studded orange will last for much longer.

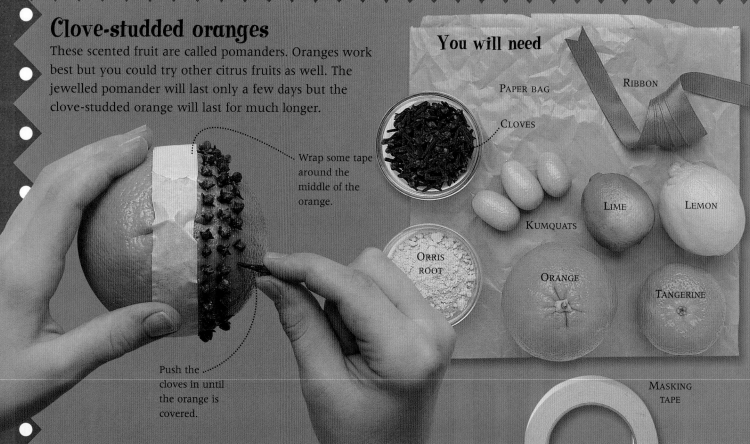

You will need

PAPER BAG

RIBBON

CLOVES

Wrap some tape around the middle of the orange.

LIME

LEMON

KUMQUATS

ORRIS ROOT

ORANGE

TANGERINE

Push the cloves in until the orange is covered.

MASKING TAPE

GROUND NUTMEG

GROUND CINNAMON

CINNAMON STICKS

FIR CONES

WHOLE CLOVES

After about six weeks your pot pourri will be ready.

Some scent tips

POT POURRI • Because the ingredients are dry it will last for ever, but the scent will fade after a few months.

POMANDERS • As the orange dries out it will shrink and only the cloves will show. It will smell nice for weeks.

ORRIS ROOT • You can buy this at health shops and pharmacies. It's used to help preserve the sweet smells.

Glass-headed pins and sequins.

Jewelled pomander

Mix up the pins and the cloves for a colourful, jewelled look.

Put the orris root into a bowl.

Wrap the orange in a paper bag.

Remove the tape and tie it up with a ribbon.

Roll the orange around until it is coated.

Tape up the top.

Leave in a warm dry place for six weeks.

33

Frosty Welcomes

Light up the night before Christmas with shining ice decorations or glistening ice-bowl lanterns.

They're illuminating!

Make your garden glow
with Christmassy candlelight

65

HOW DOES YOUR GARDEN GLOW?

All you need for a Christmas glow is some seasonal cuttings, candles, and lots of ice. You can use anything wintery for your foliage, from holly and ivy to rosehips and cranberries – just get outside, get picking, and create a welcoming light outside in your garden.

✦ The Big Freeze

Position a small bowl inside a larger one and tape it so that it is hanging in the centre – not touching the bottom or sides. Fill it with foliage and water, and freeze it.

If the small bowl bobs up too much, put some pebbles in it to weigh it down.

✦ Defrost Tip

To remove the bowls, you may have to dip the frozen lantern in warm water, and pour a little into the smaller bowl as well, to loosen the ice

✦ Ice Light

Use half a plastic bottle and a cup for the long lanterns, making sure that the cup doesn't touch the edges of the bottle at all. Use small or tall candles for the inside and if it starts to defrost, perk it up by putting it back into the freezer for a while.

Ask an adult . . .

✦ to light the candles

1

2

Let it all hang out in the garden

Tape the string to the sides of the lid to stop it from moving while it freezes.

⭐ Ice Art

Find a lid or a tray with at least a 1 cm ($1/2$ in) tall rim and fill it with water. Put your plant decorations into it then drape the ends of a long piece of string in either side – they will freeze with the ice and can be used to hang it up.

Fill up with water

Freeze it all up

4

5

Let it glow

cards and gifts

Make some glitter cards and send 3-D greetings to your friends. Print some special wrapping paper and create some pots and boxes to put your Christmas gifts in.

Glittery greetings

Pour on the glitter

and send a Christmas card with added sparkle to your special friends.

Get out your glitter

Collect up all the sparkly
things you can find:

Glitter • Glitter glue pens

Sequins • Wobbly eyes • Stickers

Gift ribbons • Tinsel

You'll also need thin card, a paintbrush,
and some PVA glue.

Conjure up a glitter card

Paint brush

PVA glue

Fold a piece of thin card in half.

Paint your design with glue.

Sprinkle on the glitter.

Put down a sheet of newspaper to catch the glitter.

Shake it off.

Finish your card with extra decoration such as stickers or paint.

Don't waste any!

Fold the newspaper in half.

Pour the glitter back.

Cookie cutter shapes

Any shape cutter will work

PVA glue

Dip a cutter in glue, press it on the paper, then cover it with glitter.

Christmas
Greetings

Greetings

From the 3rd Dimension

Bouncing Rudolphs, sticking-out snowmen,
leaping stars, and a Santa bearing a bouncing gift.

They're out of this world!

Merry Christmas

Have a cracking Christmas!

HOW TO MAKE 3-D GREETINGS

Make sure your card is the first to be noticed on the mantlepiece with these pop-up, springing, wobbling, greetings cards!

Open it up and out it pops

Template

These templates are for the Christmas tree, the snowman, and the parcels. Cut the solid lines and fold the dotted lines. Trace them onto your folded card.

Be careful not to draw your picture over half way across the card or the fold will stick out too much when the card is closed.

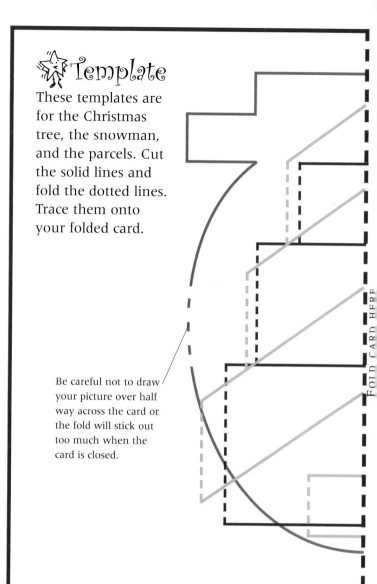

FOLD CARD HERE

3-D, Festive, Fold-out Card

From a flat card to a pile of presents in a Christmas flash! Four simple cuts and your greetings cards are transformed. Try the snowman and Christmas tree designs too.

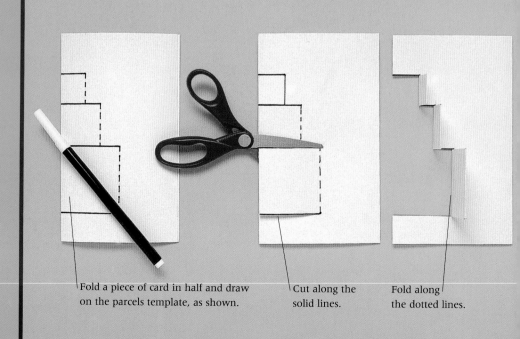

Fold a piece of card in half and draw on the parcels template, as shown.

Cut along the solid lines.

Fold along the dotted lines.

☆ Pop-up Wobble Card

With this magic spring card, you can make anything appear to jump out at the person who receives it – from Rudolph's nose to Santa's parcel or a twinkling star. Try out some of your own designs. How about some springing, jangling bells, or a snowman spring?

Rudolph's nose.

Cut out a piece of card and fold it in half.

Cut Rudolf's face and nose out of two other colours of card or paper. Glue the face onto the main card.

Help Rudolph's nose wibble and wobble!

Draw a swirl on a piece of thin card – no bigger than Rudolph's nose – and cut it out.

Glue the centre of the spring to the back of the nose.

Glue the other end of the spring to Rudolph's face.

Finish Rudolph off by drawing on his features.

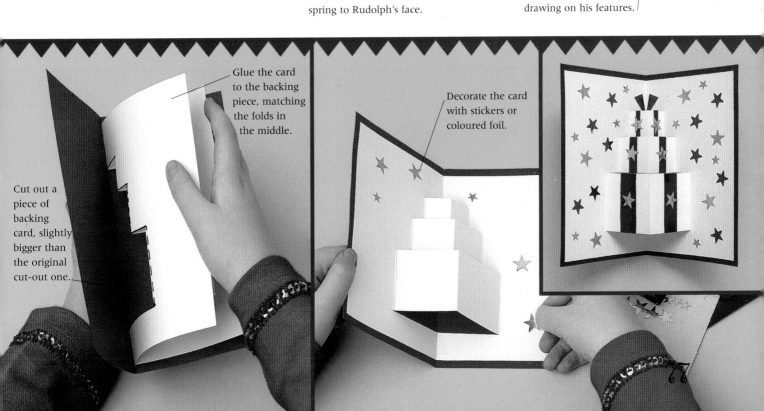

Glue the card to the backing piece, matching the folds in the middle.

Cut out a piece of backing card, slightly bigger than the original cut-out one.

Decorate the card with stickers or coloured foil.

Special gifts

Wrap and tag

Dip it, print it, wrap it, tag it!
It's great to give gifts but
even better to give them
wrapped in home-made
paper complete with
matching tags.

How to print....

Clear a space, you are now going to do some big printing! Find some plain paper that is big enough to wrap presents in – a roll of brown paper is good – and get printing. Remember to do an extra stencil that you can cut out and turn into a matching tag.

Frosty the potato man

Cut a potato in half, dab it in the paint, and press the potato onto the paper. Repeat for the body shape.

You will need:

- Sheets of plain paper
- Sponges
- Odds and ends to print with
- Acrylic paint
- Card for the stencils
- Pen and scissors
- Ribbon or string to attach the tag

Shooting star stencils

Draw a star on a piece of paper.

Cut out the star.

Place the stencil on your wrapping paper. Dip the sponge into some paint and dab it over the stencil.

Take the stencil off carefully – you don't want the paint to smudge.

Spongy festive forest

Draw your shape on a sponge.

Cut it out.

Glue the sponge onto a piece of card.

Now print your trees onto the wrapping paper and decorate them with red and gold paint.

Pen-top printing

Pen tops make pretty patterns.

Try using the eraser at the end of your pencil.

Use the base of your pen to make a big circle.

Camouflage kit

Print with a scrunched-up plastic bag to make it look like camouflage.

Marble paper

It's so good, the technique needs to be kept a secret!

Special effects

Marble paper looks so good it will astound your friends, AND it's really easy to do. Once you have made it, you can wrap things in it, cover things with it, use it as a frame, or write on it. You'll impress everyone you know!

The marble effect

Oil and water don't mix
– that's why the paint stays on the surface of the water – and that's how it makes wiggly, marbly swirls on the paper. If it doesn't make sense, don't worry, just follow the instructions – you'll be amazed.

The paint mixture

Before you start, make some pots of paint mixture in different colours. Squeeze a blob of oil paint into a pot and add four caps full of turpentine. Mix them together. The paint will become very thin.

 Ask an adult to help mix the paint with turpentine.

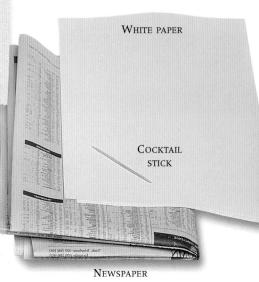

KITCHEN TOWEL

PAINT POTS

TURPENTINE

WHITE PAPER

COCKTAIL STICK

NEWSPAPER

BAKING TRAY WITH WATER

OIL PAINTS

3 Lay the paper on it
Just let the paper float on to the water.

4 Give it a prod
Gently push the paper to help it make contact.

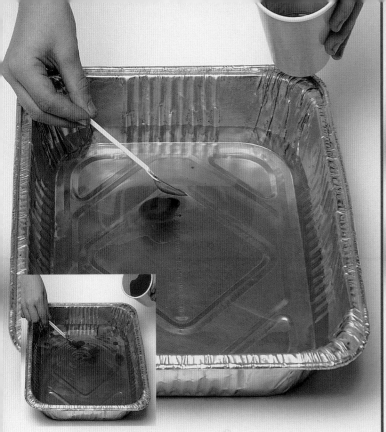

1   Add the paint to some water

Pour about 3 cm (1 in) of water into the tray. Add small spoonfuls of each colour paint mixture.

2   Swirl the paint around

With a cocktail stick, swirl the paint gently in the water, but don't mix it too well

5   Remove the paper

Pick up the corners and lift the paper out quickly.

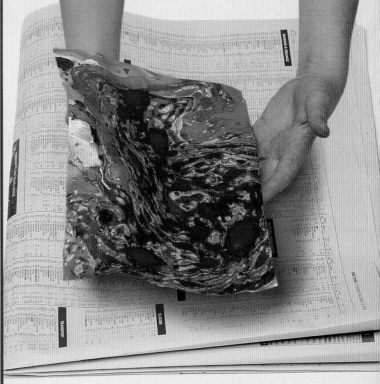

6   Leave it to dry

Allow it to dry flat on newspaper.

Printing patterns

Take plain or coloured paper and transform it into a frenzy of pattern. Go on, get printing!

Making patterns

YOU WILL NEED...

PAPER • Lots of paper to print on, such as brown packing paper, large sheets of plain white paper, or coloured paper.

PAINT • The best paint to use is poster paint but any paint you have will do.

Try these babies' footprints using your hand – you could even use your own feet.

Babies' footprints

Dip the side of your fist into some paint.

Make a print on the paper.

Use your fingertips for the toes.

Odds and ends

Search around the house for any items that you think would be good for printing. Remember to ask if you can cover them in paint first! Then dip them in the paint and press down on the paper.

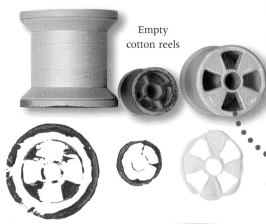

Empty cotton reels

Pen end

Scrunched up plastic or paper bag

Sponge

Cake cutters

Dip the reels into the paint.

Press down onto the paper.

Plastic letters

Carved-out carrot

Bubble wrap

Carved-out potato

Pen end

Brush

Paper boxes

What do you do if you need a box for something special? Simple
– make it yourself so you can choose the size, and the colour too.
Try using wrapping paper or home-made printed paper.

Making a block box

As you make each fold, make sure you press it down firmly so that when you open it, you can see the crease.

Cut a piece of paper into a square shape. Fold in half both ways so you have a centre point.

Fold down a corner so that it meets the centre point.

Fold the other corners into the centre.

Fold in two sides so that they reach the middle.

Unfold the two sides completely, leaving the other two corners folded in.

Fold in the two sides to the middle, and let them flap out again.

Pinch both sides of the fold – the pinches should be on a natural fold.

Bring the end right over the top.

Do the same to the other side, and tuck it in neatly...

Now all you have to do is fill your box!

Use a slightly bigger piece of paper to make a lid.

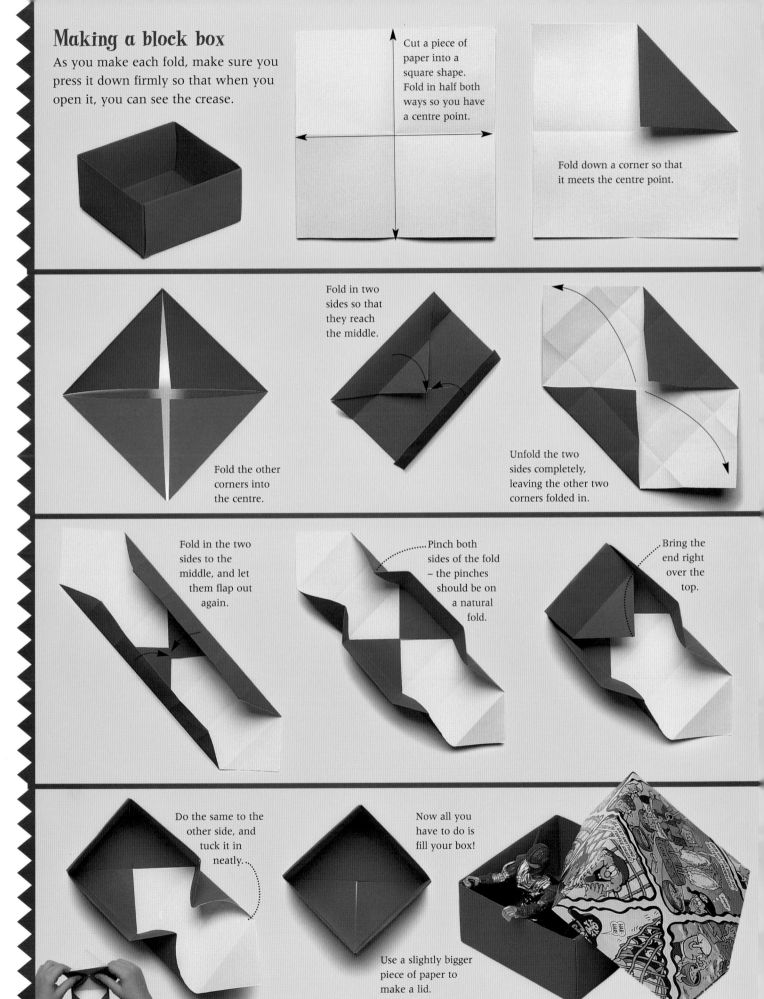

A star box

Stuff your star full of sweets and other delicious little fancies.

To start with...

fold a square piece of paper...

along each of these folds...

unfolding them again as you go.

Hold the top and bottom corners, and bring them together, making sure you tuck the two sides in.

The opening should be at the top.

It should be a diamond shape with two flaps in the middle.

Make sure the opening is at the top.

Open up the small flap and press flat.

Tuck the left side of the small flap behind itself.

Now do the same to the other side.

Fold one side along to the central fold.

Make sure these two folds line up.

Both sides should now look the same.

Turn it over so that the other side is showing.

Do the same with the flaps at the back.

Fold all four flaps down as far as they will go.

When you have folded two flaps down, pull the other two to the side and they will fold down too.

The back should look exactly the same as the front.

Your box should start to open when you fold over the flaps.

With your hand underneath, push up the middle and the final shape will miraculously appear.

Neaten up the star flaps and FILL IT UP!

Try different sizes and colours. You could even make boxes with your own printed paper.

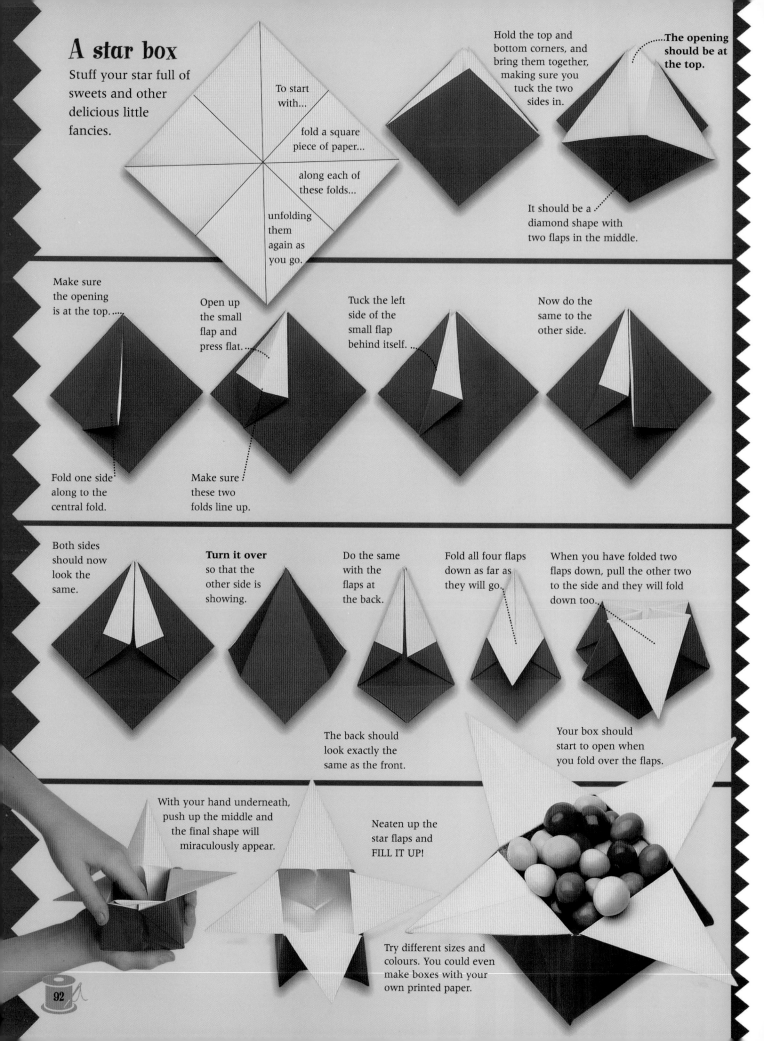

A galaxy of star boxes

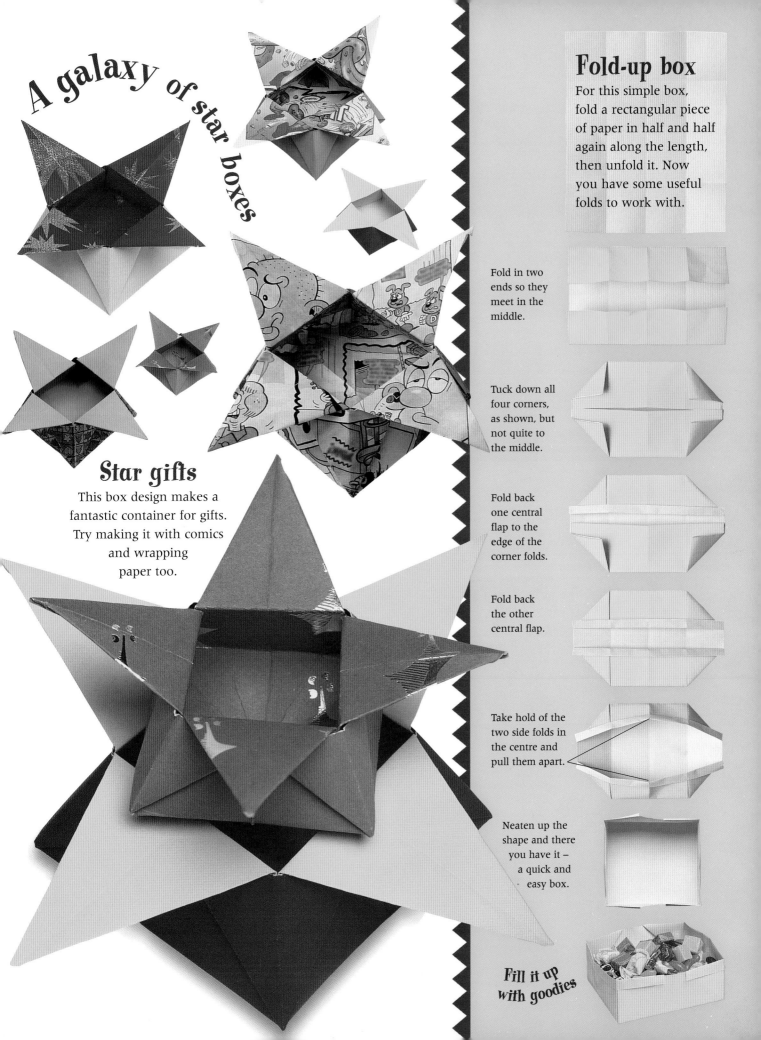

Star gifts

This box design makes a fantastic container for gifts. Try making it with comics and wrapping paper too.

Fold-up box

For this simple box, fold a rectangular piece of paper in half and half again along the length, then unfold it. Now you have some useful folds to work with.

Fold in two ends so they meet in the middle.

Tuck down all four corners, as shown, but not quite to the middle.

Fold back one central flap to the edge of the corner folds.

Fold back the other central flap.

Take hold of the two side folds in the centre and pull them apart.

Neaten up the shape and there you have it – a quick and easy box.

Fill it up with goodies

paper pots

There's paper all around you. Don't throw it away, recycle it!

Sweet wrappers

Coloured foil

Envelopes

Coloured paper

Comics

Magazines

Newspaper

How to make a pot

Vaseline

1. Blow up a balloon, spread vaseline over it, brush over some paste, and half cover it with paper.

See page 46 for more about paste.

Wallpaper paste

2. Cover the balloon with about six layers. Leave it to dry in a warm place.

3. Take the balloon out and trim off the rough edges.

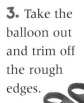

4. Make a base with a strip of card, tape it on, and cover it with paste and paper.

5. Cut card for ears, tape in place, and again cover with paste and paper.

Decorate inside and out.

Secret snowman

Surprise Surprise surprise! What's Frosty hiding under his hat?

Secret snowballs

They're not just a pretty decoration to hang on the tree, but a secret stash of goodies. Give one to a friend and fill it with gifts.

Pull your snowball apart

...and let the goodies roll out

Off with his hat!
Look what's inside

Make a paper pot

PVA GLUE

BALLOONS

TORN-UP NEWSPAPER

To stop the paper sticking to the balloon, spread vaseline over it.

1
Cover the balloon with PVA glue.

2
Spread pieces of newspaper over the balloon, leaving the bottom uncovered.

3
Repeat steps 1 and 2 six more times. Finish with a layer of PVA glue.

4
Leave it to dry for a day or two.

Use a pot to support it.

Pop!

When it's hard and dry, pop the balloon.

Make a secret snowman

You will need to start with two pots the same size. That means you will have to blow up your balloons to match. One will be for the hat and the other for the head.

2
HAT   HEAD

Trim them down

1
The dotted lines show where to trim them down.

First make two pots

FOLD ALONG DOTTED LINES

Nose template
Trace this nose shape and cut it out of card.

Paint and PVA
Mix equal amounts of paint with PVA glue. This gives a nice sheen when it has dried and makes the pot stronger.

3

MASKING TAPE

Scrunch up some paper into a ball.

Wrap it in masking tape.

Use a strong glue to fix it in place.

Make a bobble

4

Stick on a folded card nose with strong glue.

Paste some pieces of paper over the joins.

Add a nose

5

Paint them with white paint mixed with PVA glue.

Leave them to dry.

Paint them all white

6

Mix the paints with PVA glue.

Give him a face

Make a bauble

Make two pots and this time blow up two smaller balloons to the same size.

1 Make two small pots.

2 Trim them down.

Cover with white paint.

BASE POT

POT LID

3 **Ask an adult** to make a small hole in the bottom of each pot.

4 Decorate the pots with paint and glitter.

5 Take a piece of ribbon 60 cm (22 in) long and tie the two ends together.

Pass the ribbon up through the hole in the large pot.

Push the ribbon through the hole in the lid and now you can hang it up.

A Winter Wonderland

Who would ever know

that these Christmassy characters in their wintery lands are more than just great-looking faces? Open them and see for yourself.

Hats off to penguins with presents!

Keep your head or you'll give away the secret!

Goodies Galore

Don't just build one snowman, make a whole family to guard the presents and keep extra presents safely inside. Create a forest of trees in a snowy land, filled to the brim with gifts and goodies.

The penguin and snowman chat happily, keeping their secrets under their hats!

HOW TO MAKE GIFT BOXES

Collect all sorts of tubes, big or small, fat or thin, from crisp boxes and biscuit tubes to toilet and kitchen rolls – all are perfect for your character boxes. The important thing is to fill them with sweets, or other little gifts, and surprise someone on Christmas Day.

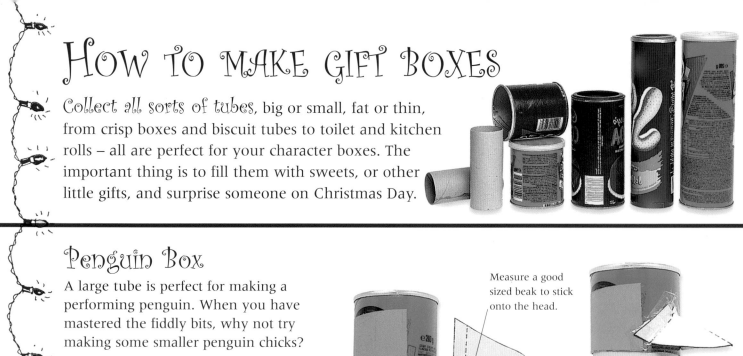

Penguin Box

A large tube is perfect for making a performing penguin. When you have mastered the fiddly bits, why not try making some smaller penguin chicks?

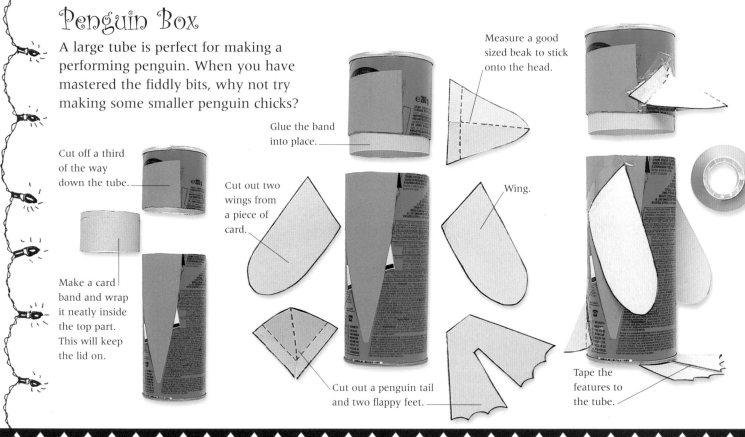

Cut off a third of the way down the tube.

Make a card band and wrap it neatly inside the top part. This will keep the lid on.

Glue the band into place.

Cut out two wings from a piece of card.

Measure a good sized beak to stick onto the head.

Wing.

Cut out a penguin tail and two flappy feet.

Tape the features to the tube.

Festive Firs

Hang these trees up by their ribbons or sit them in a foresty line-up. Why not put them around the base of a Christmas tree?

Cut a semi-circle of paper to make a cone big enough for your container.

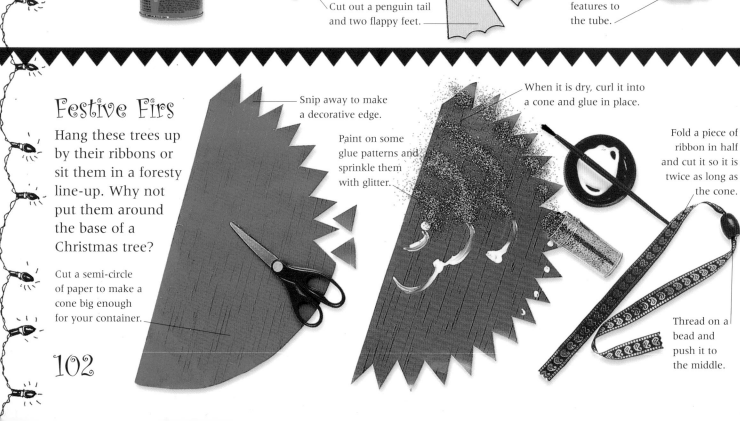

Snip away to make a decorative edge.

Paint on some glue patterns and sprinkle them with glitter.

When it is dry, curl it into a cone and glue in place.

Fold a piece of ribbon in half and cut it so it is twice as long as the cone.

Thread on a bead and push it to the middle.

102

Penguin Suit

Cut out a triangle of material.

Put glue along the edge.

Make this edge long enough to fit around the top of the head with a 5 mm (^{1}/4 in) overlap.

Try it on your penguin and trim it until it fits. Glue the sides together.

Glue the hat to the tube.

Add a band and a bobble.

Give him some eyes.

Make clothes out of scraps of material.

Paint the penguin with acrylic paint and PVA glue mixed together.

Paint the features using different colours.

Now fill up your penguin!

Dressing the Snowman

Prepare a tube in the same way as the penguin box.

Tape on pipe cleaner arms.

Spread glue on the box and cover it with tufts of cotton wool.

Put a ribbon through the lid and tape it in place.

Try making a junior snowman with a small tube.

Decorate him with material scraps.

Cover a container with gift wrap for the trunk of the tree.

Make a small hole in the top and thread the ribbon through it.

Pierce two holes in the container and tie the two ribbon ends through them.

Pop on the lid to keep the goodies locked up.

A forest of firs . . .

. . . filled with fancies

103

Packing Presents

It's the night before Christmas and as dusk falls stockings are waiting to be filled through the night. So surprise Santa with these bright ones!

Attach a tag to the top so that you can hang it up.

Stick all of the decorations on with a fabric glue. It will say on the tube if it is suitable.

Cut out two sock shapes and stick them together with a fabric glue.

Make them big, Santa's stuffing more in this year!

Cut Rudolph's face shape out of felt and stick it to the stocking. Use different colours for the features.

⭐ A Stitch in Time

To jazz up the stocking, try your hand at blanket stitch around the edges.

Start the stitch by putting the needle through about 1 cm (¹/2 in) away from the edge.

Bring the thread under the needle as you pull it down and through – it's as simple as that!

Fill me up to the brim

✰ Stick 'em Up!

If the stockings are ready then it's almost Christmas Day. Hurray! Hang it up and wait for Santa, or you could make one as a gift for someone special.

These felt snowflakes prove that you don't have to use a lot of colours to get a great Christmas look.

The best thing about these stockings is that you can use them year after year.

Making sweet treats

Chocolate Rudolphs

Melt the chocolate over a bowl of hot water.

Fill the bowl with boiling water.

Ask an adult to help with the hot water.

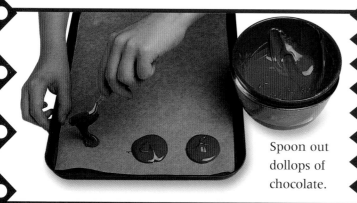

Spoon out dollops of chocolate.

Before the chocolate sets, add Rudolph's face.

Leave them to set.

Minty snowballs

Separate an egg.

Place an eggcup over the yolk.

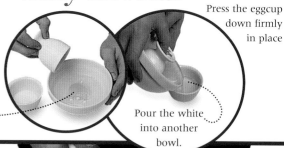

Press the eggcup down firmly in place

Pour the white into another bowl.

Whisk up the egg white.

Stop whisking before the egg white gets too stiff.

Add four teaspoons of peppermint.

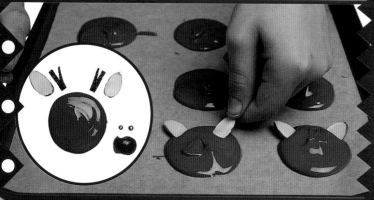

Add the egg white to the sugar.

Mix it all together.   Make into a ball.

The snowballs will be the size of large marbles.

Leave them to harden overnight.

Cut up the ball.   Make some snowballs.

Make some gifts

Use the projects in the book to create presents for your family and friends.

.....Up, up, and away

Chilly treats

Pop your biscuits into an air-tight biscuit tin and they will last a few weeks longer.

These secret pots can hold whatever you want. Keep the snowman and bring him out year after year.

Gifts to eat

Decorate a biscuit tin and fill it with your spicy stars • A felt stocking can be be filled with goodies and hung on the tree • Wrap up some minty snowballs in a cellophane bundle • Fill the snowmen with anything you want to give away

Leave the top of the sock open.

Festive fortune

Pot pourri will keep its scent if locked in a jar until it's time to give it away.

Fill woolies with dried lavender and sew up as shown on page 25.

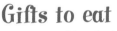

You could fill a plastic bag with your mints.

Minty bundle

Gather it up at the top and tie with a ribbon.

Scented gifts

Decorate a jar of pot pourri with a bright, festive ribbon • Present pomanders in pretty boxes plumped up with tissue or material and finished off with a ribbon • Stuff your felt shapes with dried lavender for a scented decoration

Pretty pomander sits in a posh box.

Remember, the more cloves you use the longer your pomanders will last.

Find a box your size

and ask an adult . . . .

to cut three holes in it
for your arms and head

Pass the Parcel

Do you have a
Christmas hat?
If so, put it on!

Decorate a hair
band with tinsel
for an extra
sparkle.

If you can fit your
whole body into the
box, it makes a very
cunning disguise.

Finish off
your outfit
by carrying
another
parcel – you
could fill it
with goodies.

108

All you need is a cardboard box to create a parcel party-piece to parade around in!

⭐ Wrap it Up

When you have your arm and head holes, simply wrap up the box using a roll of gift wrap and sticky tape.

⭐ Ribbons and Bows

To make ribbons and bows, cut long strips of paper and tape them around the box. Fold some extra strips into bow shapes and tape into position.

If you find a big enough box, keep your head inside and make a peep hole at the front.

Why not wear a red Christmas outfit underneath your box?

109

That's Entertainment!

Family and friends like nothing more than to sit back, relax, and be entertained. So spoil them with a spectacular show.

You're a Star

Abracadabra!

Hey Presto!

Know any magic tricks? If so, then create a magician's costume and astonish your audience. If not, then tell a few jokes or a made-up story.

I'll sing you a song

A Bit of a Song and Dance

Sing a few old favourites and encourage the audience to join in, or try your hand at one of the latest songs in the charts. When you have perfected the music, put a dance routine to it.

Carol Singers

There's nothing better at Christmas than a good sing-along of the carols that everyone knows. Perform them at home or persuade an adult to take you out on a tour of the neighbourhood. You could collect money for a charity of your choice.

Hark the Herald Angels Sing . . .

What a Performance!

⭐ **Curtains Up!**

Perform a play to your family
and friends using various props and costumes.
Try a puppet show using some old socks.

A round of applause for . . .

⭐ **That's Show Business!**

Making costumes is easier than you think, all you have
to do is search around your house for odds and ends and
use your imagination. You can create a pantomime horse
with a rug and a cardboard box, or a fairy with a ballet
outfit and a few home-made props. Invent your own
story or simply use an old favourite.

Hocus pocus, turn into a horse!

Welcome to the Christmas Quiz

Try hosting a game show for
your family. Invent your
own catch-phrases and give
away prizes – tempt the
contestants with them at the
beginning of the show. Make
up some questions or simply
ask them to race each other
with simple tasks.

Take your seats please

The Christmas Show

Performed by:
The Festive players

Act One: Aunty Jane arrives
Act Two: Disaster Dessert
Interval
Act Three: Jamie saves the day!
Grand Finale

Draw your own programme
for a show. Why not pretend
to be members of your family
and act out a family scene. Be
careful not to upset anyone!

Eats and treats

Tuck into some angel cookies and rainbow cakes, bake some bread dough shapes, and whisk up a meringue mountain for the ultimate festive feast.

Sugar and spice

Yum Yum

Spicy biscuits
With a hint of orange, dipped in sweet icing.

115

Mix up some spice

Stir up the spice - these delicious biscuits can be served up straight away or can be stored in an airtight tin for a few weeks.

ASK AN ADULT to help with the oven.

Set the oven to 190°C/375°F/Gas mark 5

Sugar

Butter

Mix them together to a creamy mixture.

1 Cream together

Add all the ingredients.

Flour

Orange rind

Cinnamon

Ginger

2 Add the flavour

3 Mix it all up

Squeeze the mixture into a ball.

Wrap the ball in a plastic bag and put in the fridge for two hours.

4 Make a ball

Sprinkle some flour on the table.

Cut the ball in half.

Roll out the dough to 5 mm (¼ in) thick.

Cut out some shapes.

5 Roll it out

Make holes for ribbons with a straw.

Place the shapes on a baking tray.

Put in the oven and bake for 15 minutes.

6 Shape and bake

You will need:

170 g (6oz) BUTTER   85 g (3oz) BROWN SUGAR   200 g (7oz) FLOUR   2 TEASPOONS GINGER   2 TEASPOONS CINNAMON   GRATED ORANGE RIND

7 Now decorate

Remove them from the oven and put them on a rack to cool.

Sugar and water icing

When the biscuits are cold, decorate them with icing. Mix 3 tablespoons of icing sugar and 3 teaspoons of water. Decorate with silver balls, or any other tasty decorations that you fancy.

Spoon on the icing and smooth it out.

Make a snowman biscuit

Cookie cutters

Cut two circles.   Join together.   Decorate

Sweets and treats

Tuck into minty snowballs and Rudolph chocolates all laid out on a plate, or wrap them up sweetly to give away as tasty gifts . . .

yum yum!

Chocolate Rudolphs

You will need:

HALF ALMONDS

GLACÉ CHERRIES HALVED

JELLY STRIPS

SILVER BALLS

CHOCOLATE 170 G (6 OZ)

TRAY AND GREASEPROOF PAPER

Minty snowballs

You will need:

PEPPERMINT ESSENCE

ONE EGG WHITE

340 G (12 OZ) ICING SUGAR

TRAY AND GREASEPROOF PAPER

Santa's on the Move

Jingle bells! Santa's on his way. Give him a little time to fill his sleigh with goodies and he'll be up in the sky in a flash.

✦ Sweet Factory

All it takes to create Santa's chalet and sleigh are lots of goodies and lots of imagination. When you have built your sleigh, fill it up with bundles of bright sweets – don't be tempted to eat them – and display them on the Christmas table.

Sugar snow sprinkled through a paper doily provides a snowy landscape for the reindeer to visit

HOW TO BUILD SANTA'S CHALET AND SLEIGH

All you need is a piece of cardboard as the sleigh base and a milk carton for the chalet.

Sugary Glue

Mix icing sugar and water to make a sticky paste. Spread it on with a knife and press your biscuits down on top of it.

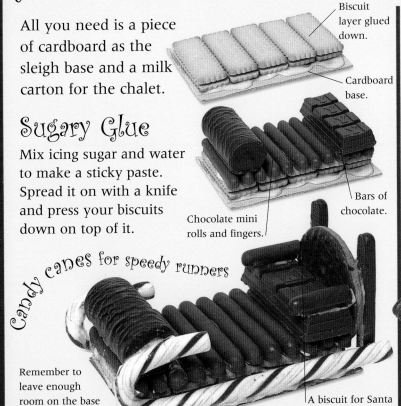

Biscuit layer glued down.

Cardboard base.

Bars of chocolate.

Chocolate mini rolls and fingers.

Candy canes for speedy runners

Remember to leave enough room on the base for the runners.

A biscuit for Santa to rest his back on.

Cut off the bottom of the carton if it is too tall.

Paste on chocolate fingers as logs for the house.

A biscuit makes a good front to start building on.

Sticky Tip

If your roof keeps slipping down, pop the box into the fridge for a few minutes to let the icing harden.

Jelly beans and hard gums are great for decoration.

Host of Angels

Heavenly biscuits adorn the table during the Christmas feast and angelic paper plates flutter gracefully around the sparkling Christmas tree.

Angel Food

250 g (9 oz) plain flour
125 g (4^1/$_2$ oz) butter
60 g (2 oz) caster sugar

Put all of the ingredients into a bowl and rub them together with your fingers to make crumbs. Slowly knead together to make a ball.

Cook for 10-15 mins (160°C/320°F/ Gas mark 3).

Crush boiled sweets and put them into the centre before you cook them for a stained glass look.

Roll out the pastry to about 1 cm (^{1}/$_3$ in) thick.

Cut a template out of card and use it to cut out the shapes.

Cut a hole in the centre of the angels.

Use cocktail sticks to make patterns.

Silver sugar balls are great for extra decoration.

Angelic Plates

Cut out the shape

Staple the skirt

Decorate the angel

Flying Angels

A host of cherubs and angels float dreamily through the sky on Christmas night. Attach a piece of string to the paper angels so that you can hang them up on branches. Let the heavenly biscuits cool and delight your family with your celestial snacks.

Santa's Sweet Factory

Yum Yum

Ho, ho, ho, Santa's been busy rustling up some tasty truffles to tickle the tastebuds.

Ask an adult . . to melt the butter

Rudolf's Truffles

125 g (4¹/₂ oz) melted butter
250 g (9 oz) crushed digestive biscuits
4 tablespoons coconut
4 tablespoons cocoa
4 tablespoons honey

Mix all the ingredients together in the pan

Crush the biscuits in a bag

Easy Peasy

The best thing about the truffles is that once the butter has melted there's no more cooking. Ask an adult to melt the butter while you crush the biscuits. Let the pan cool before you add the rest of the ingredients.

Wash your hands . . before you touch the mixture

Pour the mixture into a tray

Divide the mixture into squares with a knife.

Place the tray into a fridge for a few hours.

Roll the squares into balls

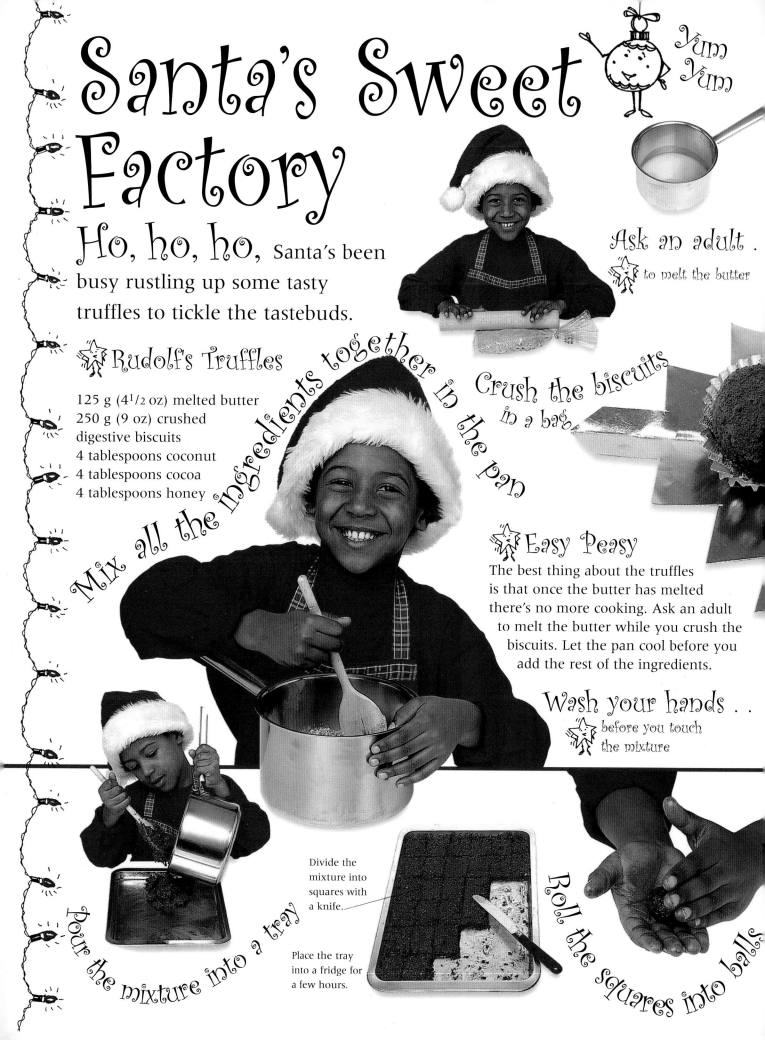

Magic Marzipan

To make truffle Santas, mix some drops of food colouring into a little marzipan, and squash into Santa's features. Shape some holly leaves and berries as decoration for the plate.

squeeze, roll, and squash into santa's features

Cover your truffles with delicious decoration

Coconut, chopped nuts, cocoa, or grated chocolate – anything you can think of!

Roll the truffles and pop them into a paper case.

125

Play dough

Have fun with bread dough: Squeeze and shape it, watch it grow – then eat it hot from the oven.

To make your dough collect these ingredients

7 g (1 sachet) easy blend yeast

750 g (1¹/2 lb) strong white flour

450 ml (³/4 pint) warm water

1 tsp salt

2 tsp sunflower oil

Makes about 10 plain rolls

Shine up your shapes by brushing them with beaten egg

To decorate your dough

1 beaten egg

Sunflower seeds

Poppy seeds

Currants and raisins

126

1. Mix it all up
Put the yeast, flour, warm water, salt, and oil into a bowl and mix them together.

2. Take the mixture out
Sprinkle the worktop with flour and take the mixture out of the bowl.

3. Start kneading
To knead, press your fist hard into the dough, then turn it and do it again.

How to make play dough

Have some fun playing with your bread dough. You'll really love to squeeze it. Squish it around, roll it into shapes, then decorate it by making a whole bread family. Watch it grow and when it's baked, serve it up hot with butter. Yum!

7. Place on a greased tray
Make sure you place the shapes far apart from each other.

8. Leave them to rise
Cover the tray loosely with clingfilm and leave it in a warm place. Leave it until it's double its size – about 30 minutes.

4. Keep kneading
Knead for 10 minutes
The dough should be stretchy, not sticky.

5. Cut up the dough
Divide the dough into smaller pieces
or pull off chunks to play with.

6. Have a play
Choose a design – try making faces.

⭐ Set the oven to
220°C/425°F/Gas mark 7

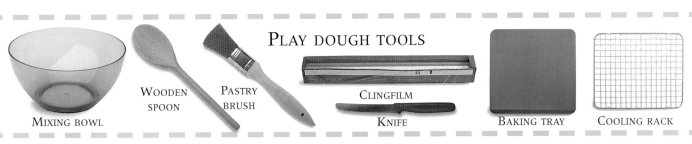

PLAY DOUGH TOOLS

MIXING BOWL WOODEN SPOON PASTRY BRUSH CLINGFILM KNIFE BAKING TRAY COOLING RACK

9. Brush on egg and decorate
Brush the bread with beaten egg and decorate with seeds.

10. Bake your bread
⭐ Bake for 10-15 minutes. The small shapes
will cook quicker, so take them out sooner.

Rainbow cakes

Heaps of colourful rainbow cakes cover the party table.

Bake little cakes and decorate them however you like.

Add your own fairy cake magic!

Magic up some fairy cakes
A measure, a whisk, or the swish of a wand.

125 g (4 oz)
self-raising flour

125 g (4 oz)
butter (room
temperature)

125 g (4 oz)
castor sugar

1 tsp baking powder

2 eggs

1 tsp vanilla essence

:) Makes 24 little cakes

LITTLE CAKE UTENSILS

MIXING BOWL

TEASPOON

TABLESPOON

SIEVE

ELECTRIC WHISK

COOLING RACK

2 BUN TINS

Fill them with paper cake cases

Rainbow icing

Mix up lots of little bowls of different coloured icing.
For green icing, mix yellow and blue; for orange,
mix yellow and red. Use anything sweet to decorate
the tops, such as glacé cherries, raisins, sweets, etc.

:) To ice 4 cakes

1 tbsp icing sugar
1 tsp water
1 drop food colouring

1. Stir together the water, food colouring, and icing sugar.

2. Drop a small dollop of icing into the centre of the cake and let it spread.

3. Decorate it with anything sweet, and use tubes of writing icing for extra patterns.

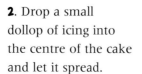

Sieving adds more air

1. Sieve the flour and baking powder

⭐ Set the oven to 190°C/375°F/Gas mark 5

5. Fill up the cases

Put a teaspoon of mixture in each case

🕐 Bake in the oven for 20 minutes.

2. Add everything else

Beat the eggs and throw them in with the butter, sugar, and vanilla essence.

3. Whisk until it's creamy

4. Does it drop off a spoon?

If it drops off easily in a dollop, then it's ready.

6. Take out of the oven

⭐ Ask an adult to help with the hot oven.

Shhh... cakes cooling

create and bake

Bake me!

make more of your cookie dough – roll it out, cut out some shapes, then have fun with icing.

cookie dough
See page 8

Makes about 24 cookies

1. Roll out the dough

Sprinkle flour on your work surface and a rolling pin. Now roll out your dough until it's 5 mm (¼ in) thick, then choose your cookie cutters and get shaping!

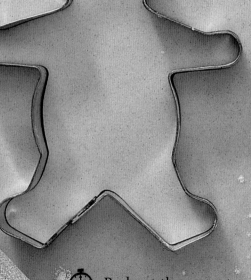

Preheat the oven to 170°C/325°F/ Gas mark 3 **!**

2. Ready to bake

Grease a baking tray and place your shapes on it, leaving spaces between them.

Bake for 15 minutes

3. Cool off

Carefully remove the tray from the oven, let them cool a little on the tray, then transfer to a cooling rack.

Tip - If it is difficult to roll, cut the ball of dough in half, and roll out one half at a time.

Ice and sprinkle

Icing – Mix up some icing sugar and water with drops of food colouring.

Icing Sugar
3 tablespoons

water
3 teaspoons

Food colouring

Icing mix

Put 3 tablespoons of icing sugar in a bowl, add 3 teaspoons of water, and stir it in. Add more water if the icing is too thick.

Now add some sprinkles.

Spoon the icing over the cookies and decorate them.

Adding colour

Use a cocktail stick to add colour to the icing mix. Keep adding and stirring until it's the colour you want.

A fun-filled box of cookies

Make holes with the end of a straw. Do this before you bake the cookie.

Use a cocktail stick to make smaller features like eyes.

Cut out a shape, then use a smaller cutter to make a new shape.

meringue mountain

whisk up egg whites into sweet frothy peaks to make delicious desserts.

Egg whites
2 whites

+

Caster Sugar
125g (4oz)

=

Makes about
12 small peaks

Fruity nest

Spoon thick cream onto a nest and top it off with pieces of fruit.

Peak sandwich

Sandwich two meringue peaks together with thick cream.

Mmmmeringue

Meringues are made from egg whites mixed with sugar baked in a very cool oven until they are crunchy on the outside and soft inside – mmmm!

Serve up your meringues with cream and fruit or just on their own.

It's ready when you can turn the bowl upside-down over your head without the egg whites sliding.

Use a big clean bowl.

Use the whisk at top speed.

3 Is it ready?

1 whisk the egg whites

2 keep whisking

whisk up a mountain

whisking is fun - An electric whisk makes the egg white froth up quicker than by hand, but remember to stop it spinning before you take it out of the bowl, or you'll cover the kitchen!

Meringue hints and tips

• Whisk the egg whites just enough – try the "over the head" test as in step 3.

• Add the sugar a tablespoon at a time while whisking. Keep repeating this until all the sugar is used up.

• Grease the tray first to stop the paper slipping.

Grease the tray then cover with greaseproof paper.

Preheat the oven to 140°C/275°F/ Gas mark 1

7 Spoon out some peaks

Pour in the sugar – about a tablespoon at a time.

4 Add some sugar and whisk

Whisk in the sugar BUT not at full speed.

5 Keep whisking

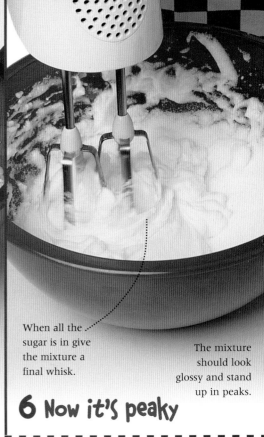

When all the sugar is in give the mixture a final whisk.

The mixture should look glossy and stand up in peaks.

6 Now it's peaky

EQUIPMENT

MIXING BOWL

ELECTRIC WHISK

TEASPOON AND DESSERT SPOON

GREASEPROOF PAPER

BAKING SHEET

PASTRY BRUSH

Press the peak down with a spoon to make a nest.

Make a snowman with peaks joined together.

 Bake in the oven for 2 hours.

8 Ready to bake

Take the meringues out of the oven.

Leave them for a few hours to dry out.

9 All dried out

Index

Acknowledgements

Dorling Kindersley would like to thank Maisie Armah, Charlotte Bull, Billy Bull, James Bull, Daniel Ceccarelli, Lulu Coulter, Seriya Ezigwe, Harry Holmstoel, Sorcha Lyons, and Kailen Wilcox for being merry models.

Additional photography: Dave King for the magician on page 110, the fairy and the pantomime horse on page 111. Steve Shott for the carol singers on pages 97 and 110.